101 BEST

SMOOTHIES & JUICES

Publications International, Ltd.

Louis Weber, CEO
Publications International, Ltd.
7373 North Cicero Avenue
Lincolnwood, IL 60712

Recipes pictured on the front cover *(left to right):* Purple Pineapple Juice *(page 142)* and Tropical Smoothie *(page 73).*
Pictured on the back cover *(left to right):* Green Islander Smoothie *(page 44)* and Apple, Tater & Carrot *(page 148).*

Cover and interior art: Dreamstime, Fotofolio, iStockphoto, PIL Collection, Shutterstock and Thinkstock.

ISBN-13: 978-1-4508-7787-9
ISBN-10: 1-4508-7787-7

Library of Congress Control Number: 2013942037

Manufactured in China.

8 7 6 5 4 3 2 1

Publications International, Ltd.

Table of Contents

Smoothies

Juices

Morning Meals

Rise & Shine Smoothie

Makes 2 servings

½ cup old-fashioned oats
1 cup orange juice
1 container (6 ounces) vanilla yogurt
½ cup vanilla soymilk
4 strawberries, hulled
3 ice cubes
1 teaspoon ground cinnamon (optional)

1. Place oats in blender; blend until fine crumbs form.

2. Add orange juice, yogurt, soymilk, strawberries, ice and cinnamon, if desired, to blender; blend until smooth.

3. Pour into two glasses. Sprinkle with additional cinnamon, if desired.

Spiced Maple Banana Oatmeal Smoothie

Makes 2 servings

½ cup ice cubes
1 frozen banana
¼ cup milk
½ cup plain yogurt
¼ cup quick oats
1 tablespoon maple syrup
⅛ teaspoon ground cinnamon
Dash ground nutmeg

1. Crush ice in blender. Add banana and milk; blend until smooth.

2. Add yogurt, oats, maple syrup, cinnamon and nutmeg; blend until smooth.

3. Pour into two glasses.

Tofu, Fruit & Veggie Smoothie

Makes 2 servings

1 cup frozen pineapple chunks
½ cup silken tofu
½ cup apple juice
½ cup orange juice
1 container (about 2½ ounces) baby food carrots

1. Combine pineapple, tofu, apple juice, orange juice and carrots in blender; blend until smooth.

2. Pour into two glasses.

Start-the-Day Smoothie

Makes 3 servings

1 package (16 ounces) frozen unsweetened peaches, partially thawed
2 containers (6 ounces each) vanilla yogurt
¾ cup white grape juice
½ teaspoon vanilla

1. Combine peaches, yogurt, grape juice and vanilla in blender; blend until smooth.

2. Pour into three glasses.

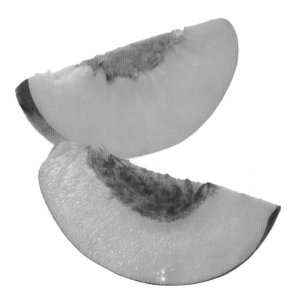

Tropical Sunrise

Makes 4 servings

1 frozen banana
1 cup frozen mango chunks
1 cup fresh pineapple chunks
⅓ cup light coconut milk
⅓ to ½ cup orange juice
1¾ cups plain nonfat yogurt

1. Combine banana, mango, pineapple, coconut milk and ⅓ cup orange juice in blender; blend until almost smooth.

2. Add yogurt; blend until smooth. Add additional orange juice to thin smoothie as desired.

3. Pour into four glasses.

. . . .

Packed with fiber, potassium and magnesium, bananas are the perfect addtion to any breakfast smoothie.

. . . .

Protein Energy Shake

Makes 4 servings

1½ cups vanilla soy yogurt
1 cup plain soymilk
¼ cup raw walnut halves
4 ice cubes
2½ tablespoons honey
¼ teaspoon ground cinnamon

1. Combine soy yogurt, soymilk, walnuts, ice, honey and cinnamon in blender; blend until smooth.

2. Pour into four glasses.

Pomegranate Breakfast Smoothie
Makes 1 serving

1 banana
½ cup mixed berries
¾ cup pomegranate juice
⅓ cup soymilk or milk

Combine banana and berries in blender; blend until smooth. Add pomegranate juice and soymilk; blend until smooth.

Cinnamon-Apple Smoothie

Makes 4 servings

2 Gala, Braeburn or other apples, peeled and sliced
2 cups ice cubes
2 bananas
1 container (6 ounces) vanilla yogurt
¾ cup apple juice
2 teaspoons ground cinnamon

1. Combine apples, ice, bananas, yogurt, apple juice and cinnamon in blender; blend until smooth.

2. Pour into four glasses.

Berry Morning Medley

Makes 2 servings

1½ cups reduced-fat (2%) milk
1 cup frozen mixed berries
½ cup plain nonfat yogurt
1 tablespoon sugar
¼ teaspoon vanilla
¼ cup granola

1. Combine milk and berries in blender; blend until smooth. Add yogurt, sugar and vanilla; blend until smooth.

2. Add granola; pulse 15 to 20 seconds to blend. Pour into two glasses.

Honeydew Ginger Smoothie

Makes 3 servings

1½ cups honeydew melon chunks
½ cup banana slices
½ cup vanilla nonfat yogurt
½ cup ice cubes (about 4)
¼ teaspoon grated fresh ginger

1. Combine honeydew, banana, yogurt, ice and ginger in blender; blend until smooth.

2. Pour into three glasses.

Superfood Smoothies

Triple Berry Blast

Makes 2 servings

1 cup frozen mixed berries
1 cup plain soymilk*
½ cup banana slices
2 teaspoons honey

Do not use vanilla soymilk; it will make this smoothie too sweet.

1. Combine berries, soymilk, banana and honey in blender; blend until smooth.

2. Pour into two glasses.

Kiwi Grape Blend

Makes 4 servings

2 cup ice cubes
1 cup green grapes
¼ honeydew melon, rind removed, seeded and
cut into chunks
4 kiwis, peeled and cut into quarters
2 tablespoons honey

1. Combine ice, grapes, honeydew, kiwis and honey in blender; blend until smooth.

2. Pour into four glasses.

Raspberry Peach Perfection

Makes 3 servings

1½ cups fresh or frozen peach slices
1 cup peach nectar
1 container (6 ounces) raspberry yogurt
¾ cup fresh or frozen raspberries
1 tablespoon honey (optional)
1 to 3 ice cubes

1. Combine peaches, nectar, yogurt, raspberries and honey, if desired, in blender; blend until smooth.

2. Add 3 ice cubes if using fresh fruit and 1 to 2 ice cubes if using frozen fruit; blend until smooth.

3. Pour into three glasses.

* * *

If your honey has crystallized, it can be easily softened in the microwave. Remove the lid and microwave the jar on HIGH about 30 seconds. Stir the honey and let stand 1 minute; repeat heating and stirring if necessary.

Anti-Stress Smoothie

Makes 4 servings

2 cups frozen blueberries
1 cup reduced-fat (2%) milk
1 cup vanilla low-fat frozen yogurt
1 banana
4 to 6 ice cubes
1 tablespoon honey

1. Combine blueberries, milk, frozen yogurt, banana, ice and honey in blender; blend until smooth.

2. Pour into four glasses.

Energy Smoothie

Makes 4 servings

1 package (16 ounces) frozen unsweetened
    strawberries, partially thawed
2 bananas
1 cup vanilla soymilk or milk*
1 container (6 ounces) lemon or vanilla yogurt
⅓ cup powdered sugar
2 teaspoons vanilla

If using milk, add 1 to 2 tablespoons additional sugar, if desired.

1. Combine strawberries, bananas, soymilk, yogurt, powdered sugar and vanilla in blender; blend until smooth.

2. Pour into four glasses.

Purplicious Pomegranate Smoothie

Makes 1 serving

1 cup frozen blueberries
½ cup pomegranate juice
½ cup raspberry sherbet
⅓ cup milk
1 to 2 tablespoons honey*

*Adjust honey depending on the sweetness of the blueberries.

Combine blueberries, pomegranate juice, sherbet, milk and honey in blender; blend until smooth.

Pumpkin Spice Smoothie

Makes 4 servings

2½ cups vanilla frozen yogurt
1 cup solid-pack pumpkin
1 cup ice cubes
2 tablespoons packed brown sugar
1 tablespoon honey
1 teaspoon pumpkin pie spice
½ teaspoon ground nutmeg

1. Combine frozen yogurt, pumpkin, ice, brown sugar, honey, pumpkin pie spice and nutmeg in blender; blend until smooth.

2. Pour into four glasses.

Mixed Berry Smoothie

Makes 3 servings

1½ cups fresh or frozen strawberries
1 cup fresh or frozen blueberries
1 cup apple juice
1 container (6 ounces) mixed berry or vanilla yogurt
½ cup fresh or frozen raspberries
1 to 3 ice cubes

1. Combine strawberries, blueberries, apple juice, yogurt and raspberries in blender; blend until smooth.

2. Add 3 ice cubes if using fresh fruit or 1 to 2 ice cubes if using frozen fruit; blend until smooth.

3. Pour into three glasses.

Super Smoothie

Makes 1 serving

1 cup coarsely chopped kale
1 cup baby spinach
1 cup ice cubes
1 banana
½ cup apple juice

Combine kale, spinach, ice, banana and apple juice in blender; blend until smooth.

Blueberry Pineapple Smoothie

Makes 3 servings

2 cups fresh or frozen blueberries
1½ cups fresh pineapple chunks
1 cup pineapple juice
1 to 3 ice cubes

1. Combine blueberries, pineapple and pineapple juice in blender; blend until smooth.

2. Add 3 ice cubes if using fresh fruit or 1 to 2 ice cubes if using frozen fruit; blend until smooth.

3. Pour into three glasses.

Blueberries have one of the highest antioxidant contents of any fruit, and research has shown that those antioxidants may be useful in warding off heart attack, stroke and certain cancers.

Kiwi Strawberry Smoothie

Makes 2 servings

2 kiwis, peeled and sliced
1 cup frozen unsweetened strawberries
1 container (6 ounces) low-fat strawberry yogurt
½ cup low-fat (1%) milk
2 tablespoons honey

1. Combine kiwis, strawberries, yogurt, milk and honey in blender; blend until smooth.

2. Pour into two glasses.

Versatile Veggies

Green Islander Smoothie

Makes 1 serving

1 cup ice cubes
½ banana
¾ cup fresh pineapple chunks
½ cup packed torn spinach
½ cup packed stemmed kale

Combine ice, banana, pineapple, spinach and kale in blender; blend until smooth.

Refresh Smoothie

Makes 1 serving

    1 cup ice cubes
    ½ cucumber, peeled, seeded and cut into chunks
    ½ cup frozen mixed berries
    2 teaspoons sugar
       Grated peel and juice of ½ lime

Combine ice, cucumber, berries, sugar, lime peel and lime juice in blender; blend until smooth.

Go Green Smoothie

Makes 1 serving

1½ cups ice cubes
1 cup packed torn spinach
½ cup vanilla almond milk
¼ cup vanilla low-fat yogurt
¼ avocado, peeled
1 teaspoon lemon juice
1 teaspoon honey

Combine ice, spinach, almond milk, yogurt, avocado, lemon juice and honey in blender; blend until smooth.

Avocados are good for more than just guacamole—they make a great addition to smoothies! Avocados are rich in folate, vitamin A and potassium; they also contein lutein, an antioxidant that helps maintain healthy eyes and skin.

Taste of Winter Smoothie

Makes 2 servings

  1 cup ice cubes
½ cup canned yams in light syrup, drained
½ cup apple cider
  1 teaspoon maple syrup
¼ teaspoon ground cinnamon

1. Combine ice, yams, apple cider, maple syrup and cinnamon in blender; blend until smooth.

2. Pour into two glasses.

Spa Smoothie

Makes 2 servings

1 cup ice cubes
½ cucumber, peeled, seeded and cut into chunks
½ cup cantaloupe chunks
½ cup sliced fresh strawberries
¼ cup plain nonfat Greek yogurt
1 tablespoon sugar
1 teaspoon grated lemon peel

1. Combine ice, cucumber, cantaloupe, strawberries, yogurt, sugar and lemon peel in blender; blend until smooth.

2. Pour into two glasses.

Blue Kale Smoothie

Makes 1 serving

1½ cups ice cubes
1 banana
1 cup packed stemmed kale
½ cup blueberries
¼ cup vanilla low-fat yogurt

Combine ice, banana, kale, blueberries and yogurt in blender; blend until smooth.

Beet & Berry Blast

Makes 2 servings

1 cup ice cubes
½ cup canned sliced beets
½ cup frozen mixed berries
½ cup orange juice
1 tablespoon lemon juice
1 tablespoon honey

1. Combine ice, beets, berries, orange juice, lemon juice and honey in blender; blend until smooth.

2. Pour into two glasses.

Peaches & Green

Makes 1 serving

1 cup ice cubes
1 cup packed torn spinach
1 cup frozen peach slices
¾ cup vanilla almond milk
2 teaspoons honey

Combine ice, spinach, peaches, almond milk and honey in blender; blend until smooth.

. . . .

Spinach contains an amazingly rich mix of essential nutrients with antioxidant functions, including vitamins C, E and A and the minerals manganese, selenium and zinc. If you don't eat enough greens every day, try drinking them instead!

. . . .

Salad Bar Smoothie

Makes 1 serving

1½ **cups ice cubes**
½ **banana**
½ **cup fresh raspberries**
½ **cup sliced fresh strawberries**
½ **cup fresh blueberries**
½ **cup packed torn spinach**

Combine ice, banana, raspberries, strawberries, blueberries and spinach in blender; blend until smooth.

Tropical Green Shake

Makes 1 serving

    1 cup ice cubes
    1 cup packed stemmed kale
    1 cup frozen tropical fruit mix*
    ½ cup orange juice
    2 tablespoons honey or agave nectar

*Tropical mix typically contains pineapple, mango and strawberries along with other fruit.

Combine ice, kale, tropical fruit mix, orange juice and honey in blender; blend until smooth.

Tropical Treats

Morning Glory Cream Fizz

Makes 2 servings

1 banana
1 cup peeled papaya or mango chunks
1 container (6 ounces) vanilla low-fat yogurt
3 tablespoons milk
1 tablespoon honey
½ cup cold club soda or sparkling water
   Ground nutmeg (optional)

1. Combine banana, papaya, yogurt, milk and honey in blender; blend until smooth.

2. Gently stir in club soda. Pour into two glasses. Sprinkle with nutmeg, if desired.

Berry Berry Mango Smoothie

Makes 2 servings

1 mango, peeled and cut into chunks
1 cup frozen strawberries
½ cup frozen raspberries
½ cup vanilla low-fat yogurt
½ cup milk
2 tablespoons honey

1. Combine mango, strawberries, raspberries, yogurt, milk and honey in blender; blend until smooth.

2. Pour into two glasses.

Pineapple Crush

Makes 2 servings

2 ice cubes
1½ cups frozen pineapple chunks
½ cup coconut milk
½ cup milk
½ cup plain yogurt
2 teaspoons sugar
1 teaspoon vanilla

1. Crush ice in blender. Add pineapple, coconut milk, milk, yogurt, sugar and vanilla; blend until smooth.

2. Pour into two glasses.

Pineapple is a nutrient bonanza! Loaded with vitamins A and C, calcium and potassium, pinapple is also high in manganese, a mineral that is important for strong bones and connective tissue. And it's a good souce of fiber as well.

Mango-Ginger Smoothie

Makes 4 servings

2 cups fresh or jarred mango chunks
1 package (16 ounces) frozen peach slices
1 cup ice cubes
1 container (6 ounces) vanilla yogurt
2 tablespoons honey
2 teaspoons grated fresh ginger

1. Combine mango, peaches, ice, yogurt, honey and ginger in blender; blend until smooth.

2. Pour into four glasses.

Papaya-Pineapple Smoothie

Makes 2 servings

½ (20-ounce) can pineapple chunks in juice
2 cups fresh papaya chunks
1 tablespoon lime juice
1 to 2 tablespoons powdered sugar*

*Increase powdered sugar to 2 tablespoons depending on the sweetness of the papaya.

1. Drain pineapple, reserving ½ cup juice. Freeze pineapple chunks 30 minutes or until frozen.

2. Combine frozen pineapple, reserved pineapple juice, papaya, lime juice and powdered sugar in blender; blend until smooth.

3. Pour into two glasses.

Lemon Mango Smoothie

Makes 1 serving

1 cup frozen mango chunks
¾ cup mango nectar
¼ cup lemon sorbet
2 tablespoons lime juice
1 to 2 tablespoons honey*
¼ teaspoon grated lime peel

*Adjust honey depending on the sweetness of the mango.

Combine mango, mango nectar, sorbet, lime juice honey and lime peel in blender; blend until smooth.

Tropical Smoothie

Makes 2 servings

2 mangoes*, peeled and cut into chunks (1⅓ cups)
6 tablespoons fresh lime juice
3 tablespoons fat-free (skim) milk
3 tablespoons pineapple-orange juice
⅔ cup vanilla frozen yogurt

*You can substitute 1⅓ cups frozen mango chunks for the fresh mango. Partially thaw the mango before using it (microwave on LOW for 1 to 2 minutes).

1. Combine mangoes, lime juice, milk and pineapple-orange juice in blender; blend until smooth. Add frozen yogurt; blend until smooth.

2. Pour into two glasses.

Spiced Passion Fruit Smoothie

Makes 2 servings

1 cup vanilla nonfat Greek yogurt
1 cup sliced fresh strawberries
1 banana
¼ cup thawed frozen passion fruit juice concentrate
¾ teaspoon pumpkin pie spice
⅛ teaspoon white pepper

1. Combine yogurt, strawberries, banana, passion fruit juice concentrate, pumpkin pie spice and white pepper in blender; blend until smooth.

2. Pour into two glasses.

Cuban Batido

Makes 2 servings

1½ cups fresh pineapple chunks
1 cup ice cubes
¾ cup milk
½ cup orange juice
3 tablespoons sugar
1 tablespoon lime juice

1. Combine pineapple, ice, milk, orange juice, sugar and lime juice in blender; blend until smooth.

2. Pour into two glasses.

Strawberry Banana Coconut Smoothie

Makes 3 servings

2 cups fresh or frozen strawberries
1¼ cups unsweetened canned coconut milk
1 teaspoon rum extract (optional)
1 banana
1 to 3 ice cubes

1. Combine strawberries, coconut milk and rum extract, if desired, in blender; blend until smooth.

2. Add banana; blend until smooth. Add 3 ice cubes if using fresh fruit and 1 to 2 ice cubes if using frozen fruit; blend until smooth.

3. Pour into three glasses.

When purchasing fresh strawberries, look for berries that are shiny, bright red and fragrant, with green caps that are vibrant in color. Green or pale red berries are underripe and will never ripen any further.

Healthful Indulgences

Strawberry Sundae Smoothie

Makes 4 servings

  3 cups ice
10 ounces frozen unsweetened strawberries, thawed
  1 cup milk
  ¾ cup plain low-fat yogurt
  2 bananas
  2 tablespoons sugar

1. Combine ice, strawberries, milk, yogurt, bananas and sugar in blender; blend until smooth.

2. Pour into four glasses.

Peanut Butter Smoothie

Makes 4 servings

2 cups vanilla low-fat frozen yogurt
2 bananas
2 cups ice cubes
1 cup fat-free (skim) milk
1 cup creamy peanut butter
2 tablespoons honey

1. Combine frozen yogurt, bananas, ice, milk, peanut butter and honey in blender; blend until smooth.

2. Pour into four glasses.

Lemon Melon Crème Smoothie

Makes 3 servings

3 cups honeydew melon chunks
½ (12-ounce) can frozen lemonade concentrate,
thawed
2 tablespoons low-fat vanilla yogurt

1. Combine honeydew, lemonade concentrate and yogurt in blender; blend until smooth.

2. Pour into three glasses.

Raspberry Chocolate Smoothie

Makes 3 servings

2 cups fresh or frozen raspberries
¾ cup milk
1 container (6 ounces) vanilla yogurt
3 tablespoons chocolate syrup
1 to 3 ice cubes

1. Combine raspberries, milk, yogurt and chocolate syrup in blender; blend until smooth.

2. Add 3 ice cubes if using fresh fruit and 1 to 2 ice cubes if using frozen fruit; blend until smooth.

3. Pour into three glasses.

Purchase extra raspberries when they are in season so you can enjoy them in smoothies year round. To freeze, spread them in a single layer on a jelly-roll pan and freeze until firm. Then transfer them to a freezer bag or airtight container.

Carrot Cake Smoothie

Makes 4 servings

4 containers (4 ounces each) baby food carrots
1 cup vanilla low-fat frozen yogurt
½ cup reduced-fat (2%) milk
¼ cup sugar
2 ice cubes
½ teaspoon ground cinnamon
⅛ teaspoon ground ginger
   Dash ground nutmeg
   Dash salt

1. Combine carrots, frozen yogurt, milk, sugar, ice, cinnamon, ginger, nutmeg and salt in blender; blend until smooth.

2. Pour into four glasses.

Blueberry Cherry "Cheesecake" Smoothie

Makes 3 servings

2 cups fresh or frozen blueberries
1¼ cups milk
½ cup fresh or frozen cherries
¼ cup (2 ounces) cream cheese
1 to 3 ice cubes

1. Combine blueberries, milk, cherries and cream cheese in blender; blend until smooth.

2. Add 3 ice cubes if using fresh fruit and 1 to 2 ice cubes if using frozen fruit; blend until smooth.

3. Pour into three glasses.

Dreamsicle Smoothie

Makes 4 servings

2 cups ice cubes
1½ cups vanilla yogurt
¾ cup thawed frozen orange juice concentrate
½ cup milk
¼ teaspoon vanilla

1. Combine ice, yogurt, orange juice concentrate, milk and vanilla in blender; blend until smooth.

2. Pour into four glasses.

"Hot" Chocolate Smoothie

Makes 4 servings

2½ cups chocolate low-fat frozen yogurt
1¾ cups chocolate soymilk
1½ cups ice cubes
  1 banana
  ⅛ teaspoon chipotle chili powder

1. Combine frozen yogurt, soymilk, ice, banana and chili powder in blender; blend until smooth.

2. Pour into four glasses.

Dessert Date Smoothie

Makes 1 serving

½ cup dried pitted dates (about 10)
¾ cup vanilla frozen yogurt
1 tablespoon honey
⅛ teaspoon ground nutmeg

1. Place dates in microwavable measuring cup; add enough water to equal ½ cup. Microwave on HIGH 1 minute; let cool to room temperature.

2. Combine dates with water, frozen yogurt, honey and nutmeg in blender; blend until smooth.

Black Forest Smoothie

Makes 2 servings

1 container (6 ounces) cherry yogurt
½ cup frozen dark sweet cherries
¼ cup reduced-fat (2%) milk
2 ice cubes
2 tablespoons sugar
2 tablespoons unsweetened cocoa powder
¼ teaspoon almond extract

1. Combine yogurt, cherries, milk, ice, sugar, cocoa and almond extract in blender; blend until smooth.

2. Pour into two glasses.

Breakfast Blends

Morning Refresher

Makes 2 servings

¼ pineapple, peeled
1 orange, peeled
1 inch fresh ginger, peeled

Juice pineapple, orange and ginger. Stir.

Sunset Berry

Makes 2 servings

1 cup strawberries, hulled
1 orange, peeled
½ lime, peeled

Juice strawberries, orange and lime. Stir.

Spicy-Sweet Grapefruit
Makes 3 servings

2 grapefruits, peeled
5 carrots
1 inch fresh ginger, peeled

Juice grapefruits, carrots and ginger. Stir.

. . . .

*Tangy, low-calorie grapefruit is packed
with vitamin C, and the pink and red
varieties also offer plentiful vitamin A in
the form of beta-carotene. Grapefruit
also contains phytonutrients that help
shield the eyes from certain types of
sight-stealing eye disease.*

. . . .

Blueberry Haze

Makes 2 servings

    2 apples
1½ cups blueberries
  ½ grapefruit, peeled
   1 inch fresh ginger, peeled

Juice apples, blueberries, grapefruit and ginger. Stir.

Citrus Carrot

Makes 2 servings

1 orange, peeled
2 carrots
½ lemon, peeled

Juice orange, carrots and lemon. Stir.

Island Orange Juice

Makes 2 servings

2 oranges, peeled
2 guavas
½ cup strawberries, hulled

Juice oranges, guavas and strawberries. Stir.

Tangerapple

Makes 2 servings

2 apples
2 tangerines, peeled
¼ lemon, peeled

Juice apples, tangerines and lemon. Stir.

Pomegranate Apple

Makes 2 servings

2 pomegranates, peeled
2 apples

Juice pomegranate seeds and apples. Stir.

Tropical Twist

Makes 2 servings

⅛ **pineapple, peeled**
⅛ **seedless watermelon, rind removed**
 1 **orange, peeled**
½ **mango, peeled**
⅓ **cup strawberries, hulled**

Juice pineapple, watermelon, orange, mango and strawberries. Stir.

Red Orange Juice

Makes 2 servings

1 orange, peeled
1 apple
½ cup raspberries
½ cup strawberries, hulled

Juice orange, apple, raspberries and strawberries. Stir.

Raspberries are highly perishable, so buy them within a day or two of when you plan to use them. In the meantime, place the unwashed berries in a single layer on a plate or cookie sheet, cover loosely with plastic wrap and refrigerate.

Immunity Boosters

Super C
Makes 3 servings

2 oranges, peeled
1 grapefruit, peeled
1 lemon, peeled
½ cup cranberries
2 teaspoons honey

Juice oranges, grapefruit, lemon and cranberries.
Stir in honey until well blended.

Pomegranate-Lime-Coconut Juice

Makes 2 servings

1 pomegranate, peeled
½ cucumber
1 lime, peeled
¼ cup coconut water

Juice pomegranate seeds, cucumber and lime.
Stir in coconut water until well blended.

Headache Buster

Makes 1 serving

1 cup cauliflower florets
1 cup broccoli florets
1 apple

Juice cauliflower, broccoli and apple. Stir.

Broccoli is a treasure trove of valuable nutrients, including vitamins C, E and A (mostly as the antioxidant beta-carotene), along with minerals such as calcium, folate and potassium.

Plum Cherry

Makes 2 servings

2 dark plums
1½ cups cherries, pitted

Juice plums and cherries. Stir.

Citrus Sprout

Makes 2 servings

1 cup brussels sprouts
4 leaves romaine lettuce
1 orange, peeled
½ apple
½ lemon, peeled

Juice brussels sprouts, romaine, orange, apple and lemon. Stir.

Antioxidant Cocktail

Makes 3 servings

1 grapefruit, peeled
2 oranges, peeled
½ cup blackberries

Juice grapefruit, oranges and blackberries. Stir.

Cold and Flu Ninja Juice

Makes 2 servings

1 orange, peeled
½ lemon, peeled
⅛ small red onion
1 clove garlic
½ teaspoon honey

Juice orange, lemon, onion and garlic. Stir in honey until well blended.

Joint Comfort Juice

Makes 2 servings

2 cups fresh spinach
¼ pineapple, peeled
1 pear
1 bunch fresh parsley
½ grapefruit, peeled

Juice spinach, pineapple, pear, parsley and grapefruit. Stir.

Super Berry Refresher

Makes 2 servings

1 cup strawberries, hulled
1 cup raspberries
1 cucumber
½ cup blackberries
½ cup blueberries
¼ lemon, peeled

Juice strawberries, raspberries, cucumber, blackberries, blueberries and lemon. Stir.

Cleansing Green Juice

Makes 2 servings

4 leaves bok choy
1 stalk celery
½ cucumber
¼ bulb fennel
½ lemon, peeled

Juice bok choy, celery, cucumber, fennel and lemon. Stir.

Refreshing Roots

Fiery Cucumber Beet Juice

Makes 2 servings

1 cucumber
1 beet
1 lemon, peeled
1 inch fresh ginger, peeled
½ jalapeño pepper

Juice cucumber, beet, lemon, ginger and jalapeño pepper. Stir.

Jicama Pear Carrot

Makes 1 serving

   1 cup peeled jicama chunks
   ½ pear
   2 carrots
   ½ inch fresh ginger, peeled
      Pinch ground red pepper (optional)

Juice jicama, pear, carrots and ginger. Stir in red pepper, if desired, until well blended.

Tangy Twist

Makes 3 servings

1 grapefruit, peeled
4 carrots
1 apple
1 beet
1 inch fresh ginger, peeled
   Ice cubes

Juice grapefruit, carrots, apple, beet and ginger.
Stir. Serve over ice.

Piquant Parsnip Carrot

Makes 2 servings

2 parsnips
2 carrots
½ cucumber
1 lemon, peeled

Juice parsnips, carrots, cucumber and lemon. Stir.

Purple Pineapple Juice

Makes 2 servings

1 beet
1 pear
¼ pineapple, peeled
1 inch fresh ginger, peeled

Juice beet, pear, pineapple and ginger. Stir.

Easy Being Green

Makes 2 servings

   2 cups watercress
   2 parsnips
   2 stalks celery
   ½ cucumber
   4 sprigs fresh basil

Juice watercress, parsnips, celery, cucumber and basil. Stir.

Back to Your Roots

Makes 3 servings

2 beets
2 carrots
2 parsnips
1 turnip
1 sweet potato

Juice beets, carrots, parsnips, turnip and sweet potato. Stir.

Hang Loose

Makes 1 serving

5 carrots
2 radishes
½ inch fresh ginger, peeled

Juice carrots, radishes and ginger. Stir.

Apple, Tater & Carrot

Makes 4 servings

4 apples
1 sweet potato
1 carrot

Juice apples, sweet potato and carrot. Stir.

Veggie Delight

Makes 2 servings

1 carrot
1 stalk celery
1 beet
1 apple
½ small sweet onion

Juice carrot, celery, beet, apple and onion. Stir.

. . . .

*Purchase beets that are firm, with
smooth skins and tops attached.
The beets should have a deep,
rich purple-red color, while the tops
should be fresh looking, dark green
and crisp. Choose small to medium
beets as they are usually sweeter
and more tender. Always scrub
beets and other root vegetables
thoroughly before juicing.*

. . . .

Vegetable Vitality

Amazing Green Juice

Makes 2 servings

1 cucumber
1 green apple
2 stalks celery
½ bulb fennel
3 leaves kale

Juice cucumber, apple, celery, fennel and kale.
Stir.

Triple Pepper

Makes 2 servings

2 apples
1 red bell pepper
1 yellow bell pepper
½ jalapeño pepper

Juice apples, bell peppers and jalapeño pepper.
Stir.

Tropical Veggie Juice

Makes 2 servings

5 leaves kale
⅛ pineapple, peeled
½ cucumber
½ cup coconut water

Juice kale, pineapple and cucumber. Stir in coconut water until well blended.

Orange Fennel Sprout

Makes 2 servings

2 oranges, peeled
2 stalks celery
1 bulb fennel
1 cup alfalfa sprouts

Juice oranges, celery, fennel and alfalfa sprouts.
Stir.

Apple Carrot Zinger

Makes 2 servings

    2 apples
    4 carrots
    ¼ cucumber
    1 inch fresh ginger, peeled

Juice apples, carrots, cucumber and ginger. Stir.

Green Juice

Makes 2 servings

2 cups fresh spinach
2 cucumbers
1 pear
½ lemon, peeled
1 inch fresh ginger, peeled

Juice spinach, cucumbers, pear, lemon and ginger. Stir.

Red Cabbage & Pineapple

Makes 2 servings

¼ red cabbage
¼ pineapple, peeled

Juice cabbage and pineapple. Stir.

Both red and green cabbage provide vitamin C, although the red variety has about twice as much as the green. As an antioxidant, vitamin C works to shield the body from toxins that can damage cells and contribute to cancer, heart disease and many physical signs of aging.

Mojo Mojito Juice

Makes 2 servings

1 cucumber
1 pear
1 cup fresh mint
½ lime, peeled

Juice cucumber, pear, mint and lime. Stir.

Sweet Pepper Carrot

Makes 2 servings

3 carrots
1 red bell pepper
1 yellow bell pepper

Juice carrots and bell peppers. Stir.

Mean & Green

Makes 2 servings

1 green apple
2 stalks celery
3 leaves kale
½ cucumber
½ lemon, peeled
1 inch fresh ginger, peeled

Juice apple, celery, kale, cucumber, lemon and ginger. Stir.

....

Choose firm cucumbers with smooth, vibrantly colored skins. Store unwashed cucumbers in a plastic bag in the refrigerator for up to ten days. Right before juicing, wash cucumbers thoroughly under cool running water. Tougher-skinned varieties should be peeled prior to juicing; softer-skinned cukes may simply need to be cut up to fit into the juicer.

....

Fruit Favorites

Tangerine Ginger Sipper
Makes 2 servings

1 tangerine, peeled
1 pear
¼ lemon, peeled
½ inch fresh ginger, peeled

Juice tangerine, pear, lemon and ginger. Stir.

Melon Raspberry Medley

Makes 2 servings

⅛ **honeydew melon, rind removed**
⅛ **seedless watermelon, rind removed**
½ **cup raspberries**
  Ice cubes

Juice honeydew, watermelon and raspberries. Stir. Serve over ice.

Cool Pear Melon

Makes 3 servings

¼ honeydew melon, rind removed
1 pear
½ cucumber

Juice honeydew, pear and cucumber. Stir.

Sweet & Spicy Citrus

Makes 2 servings

5 carrots
1 orange *or* 2 clementines, peeled
⅓ cup strawberries, hulled
1 lemon, peeled
½ inch fresh ginger, peeled

Juice carrots, orange, strawberries, lemon and ginger. Stir.

Melonade

Makes 4 servings

¼ seedless watermelon, rind removed
1 apple
1 lemon, peeled

Juice watermelon, apple and lemon. Stir.

Mango Tango
Makes 2 servings

1 mango, peeled
1 lime, peeled
½ lemon, peeled
Ice cubes

Juice mango, lime and lemon. Stir. Serve over ice.

Cherry & Melon

Makes 3 servings

⅛ **seedless watermelon, rind removed**
¼ **cantaloupe, rind removed**
¾ **cup cherries, pitted**

Juice watermelon, cantaloupe and cherries. Stir.

Spicy Pineapple Carrot

Makes 2 servings

½ **pineapple, peeled**
2 carrots
1 inch fresh ginger, peeled
  Ice cubes

Juice pineapple, carrots and ginger. Stir. Serve over ice.

. . . .

The bottom of a pineapple should smell sweet—but not overly so—and appear golden yellow. (Pineapples ripen from the base up, so if it smells sweet at the top, the bottom may already be overripe.) The pineapple should yield slightly when pressed but shouldn't feel soft or mushy.

. . . .

Kiwi Twist

Makes 2 servings

2 kiwis, peeled
2 pears
½ lemon, peeled

Juice kiwis, pears and lemon. Stir.

Peachy Keen

Makes 2 servings

2 peaches
1 cup red seedless grapes
¼ lemon, peeled

Juice peaches, grapes and lemon. Stir.

METRIC CONVERSION CHART

VOLUME MEASUREMENTS (dry)

¹/₈ teaspoon = 0.5 mL
¹/₄ teaspoon = 1 mL
¹/₂ teaspoon = 2 mL
³/₄ teaspoon = 4 mL
1 teaspoon = 5 mL
1 tablespoon = 15 mL
2 tablespoons = 30 mL
¹/₄ cup = 60 mL
¹/₃ cup = 75 mL
¹/₂ cup = 125 mL
²/₃ cup = 150 mL
³/₄ cup = 175 mL
1 cup = 250 mL
2 cups = 1 pint = 500 mL
3 cups = 750 mL
4 cups = 1 quart = 1 L

VOLUME MEASUREMENTS (fluid)

1 fluid ounce (2 tablespoons) = 30 mL
4 fluid ounces (¹/₂ cup) = 125 mL
8 fluid ounces (1 cup) = 250 mL
12 fluid ounces (1¹/₂ cups) = 375 mL
16 fluid ounces (2 cups) = 500 mL

WEIGHTS (mass)

¹/₂ ounce = 15 g
1 ounce = 30 g
3 ounces = 90 g
4 ounces = 120 g
8 ounces = 225 g
10 ounces = 285 g
12 ounces = 360 g
16 ounces = 1 pound = 450 g

DIMENSIONS

¹/₁₆ inch = 2 mm
¹/₈ inch = 3 mm
¹/₄ inch = 6 mm
¹/₂ inch = 1.5 cm
³/₄ inch = 2 cm
1 inch = 2.5 cm

OVEN TEMPERATURES

250°F = 120°C
275°F = 140°C
300°F = 150°C
325°F = 160°C
350°F = 180°C
375°F = 190°C
400°F = 200°C
425°F = 220°C
450°F = 230°C

BAKING PAN SIZES

Utensil	Size in Inches/Quarts	Metric Volume	Size in Centimeters
Baking or	8×8×2	2 L	20×20×5
Cake Pan	9×9×2	2.5 L	23×23×5
(square or	12×8×2	3 L	30×20×5
rectangular)	13×9×2	3.5 L	33×23×5
Loaf Pan	8×4×3	1.5 L	20×10×7
	9×5×3	2 L	23×13×7
Round Layer	8×1½	1.2 L	20×4
Cake Pan	9×1½	1.5 L	23×4
Pie Plate	8×1¼	750 mL	20×3
	9×1¼	1 L	23×3
Baking Dish	1 quart	1 L	—
or Casserole	1½ quart	1.5 L	—
	2 quart	2 L	—